Just One Pot

Just One Pot

Love Food™ is an imprint of Parragon Books Ltd.

Parragon
Queen Street House
4 Queen Street
Bath BA1 1HE, UK

ISBN 978-1-4075-0716-3

Printed in China

Photography by Mike Cooper
Home Economy by Sumi Glass and Lincoln Jefferson
Cover and internal design by Mark Cavanagh
Introduction by Linda Doeser

Notes for the reader
• This book uses imperial, metric, and U.S. cup measurements. Follow the same units of measurement throughout; do not mix imperial and metric.
• All spoon measurements are level: teaspoons are assumed to be 5 ml and tablespoons are assumed to be 15 ml.
• Unless otherwise stated, milk is assumed to be low-fat and eggs are medium-size. The times given are an approximate guide only.
• Some recipes contain nuts. If you are allergic to nuts, you should avoid using them and any products containing nuts. Recipes using raw or very lightly cooked eggs should be avoided by infants, the elderly, pregnant women, convalescents, and anyone with a chronic condition.

CONTENTS

Introduction

Mention one-pot cooking and most people will immediately think of stews and casseroles and these are, indeed, tasty, nutritious, and popular one-pot meals. However, Just one pot shows that there's far more to one-pot cooking-from cremy risottos to a hearty pot roast,and chunky soups to a flavor-packed paella.

The idea of creating diverse, flavorsome, and easy recipes is already appealing, but when you add to that the fact that all the recipes in this collection can be created in just one pot it seems too good to be true. This added bonus certainly makes clearing up afterwards less of a chore, especially as many of the dishes can be cooked and served in the same dish. Less energy is used to cook them, making a useful saving on the family budget in these days of soaring costs, as well as being environmentally friendly. This is no small consideration in today's world.

Including fortifying soups, stews, and casseroles, these one-pot meals are great weekend dishes when there is time available for an assortment of ingredients to simmer slowly until their flavors have blended lusciously together. However, everyone's life is busy these days and midweek family suppers must often be prepared and cooked quickly. Fortunately, there are a lot of equally cheering, filling, and scrumptious dishes that take little time to cook. Speedy stove-top suppers that feature warming spices—from chili to saffron—are the perfect choice to perk up an evening. Also, a lot of one-pot dishes freeze well, so if you cook double the quantity, which certainly won't take you twice the time, you can save a whole meal for another day.

The recipes in this book have been inspired by dishes from around the world. You can tuck into a Moroccan stew, a Hungarian goulash, or Spanish paella. The sheer variety of dishes—all of them packed with flavor—guarantees that there is sure to be something to suit all tastes and occasions. The recipes are divided into five chapters, starting with meal-in-a-bowl soups and then featuring meat, poultry, fish and shellfish, and vegetables respectively, so you'll never be short of ideas!

Meal-in-a-Bowl Soups

Homemade soup is the ultimate comfort food and the perfect choice for a weekend lunch at any time of year. Serve it with crusty bread or rolls and, perhaps, some cheese and you'll have a filling, well-balanced meal for all the family. There are some very good-quality bouillon powders and prepared stocks available nowadays, so it need not be a chore to rustle up a brimming bowl of soup, broth, or chowder.

Minestrone

Heat the oil in a large pan. Add the garlic, onions, and prosciutto and cook over medium heat, stirring, for 3 minutes, until slightly softened. Add the red and orange bell peppers and the chopped tomatoes and cook for another 2 minutes, stirring. Stir in the stock, then add the celery, beans, cabbage, peas, and parsley. Season to taste with salt and pepper. Bring to a boil, then lower the heat and simmer for 30 minutes.

Add the vermicelli to the pan. Cook for another 10–12 minutes, or according to the instructions on the package. Remove from the heat and ladle into serving bowls. Garnish with freshly grated Parmesan and serve with fresh crusty bread.

SERVES 4

2 tbsp olive oil

2 garlic cloves, chopped

2 red onions, chopped

$2^3/_4$ oz/75 g prosciutto, sliced

1 red bell pepper, seeded and chopped

1 orange bell pepper, seeded and chopped

14 oz/400 g canned chopped tomatoes

4 cups vegetable stock

1 celery stalk, trimmed and sliced

14 oz/400 g canned cranberry beans, drained

$3^1/_2$ oz/100 g green leafy cabbage, shredded

$2^3/_4$ oz/75 g frozen peas, thawed

1 tbsp chopped fresh parsley

salt and pepper

$2^3/_4$ oz/75 g dried vermicelli

freshly grated Parmesan cheese, to garnish

fresh crusty bread, to serve

French Onion Soup

Thinly slice the onions. Heat the oil over medium-high heat in a large, heavy-bottom pan, then add the onions and cook, stirring occasionally, for 10 minutes, until they are just beginning to brown. Stir in the chopped garlic, sugar, and thyme, then reduce the heat and cook, stirring occasionally, for 30 minutes, or until the onions are golden brown.

Sprinkle in the flour and cook, stirring, for 1–2 minutes. Stir in the wine. Gradually stir in the stock and bring to a boil, skimming off any foam that rises to the surface, then reduce the heat and simmer for 45 minutes. Meanwhile, toast the bread on both sides under a preheated medium broiler. Rub the toast with the whole garlic clove.

Ladle the soup into 6 flameproof bowls set on a cookie sheet. Float a piece of toast in each bowl and divide the grated cheese among them. Place under a preheated medium-hot broiler for 2–3 minutes, or until the cheese has just melted. Garnish with thyme and serve.

SERVES 6

1 lb 8 oz/675 g onions

3 tbsp olive oil

4 garlic cloves, 3 chopped and
   1 peeled but kept whole

1 tsp sugar

2 tsp chopped fresh thyme

2 tbsp all-purpose flour

$^1/_2$ cup dry white wine

8 cups vegetable stock

6 slices French bread

3 cups grated Swiss cheese

fresh thyme sprigs, to garnish

Mexican-style Beef & Rice Soup

Heat half the oil in a large saucepan over medium-high heat. Add the meat in one layer and cook until well browned, turning to color all sides. Using a slotted spoon, transfer the meat to a plate. Drain off the oil and wipe out the pan with paper towels.

Heat the remaining oil in the saucepan over medium heat. Add the onion, cover, and cook for about 3 minutes, stirring occasionally, until just softened. Add the green bell pepper, chile, garlic, and carrot, and continue cooking, covered, for 3 minutes.

Add the coriander, cumin, cinnamon, oregano, bay leaf, and orange rind. Stir in the tomatoes and stock, along with the beef and wine. Bring almost to a boil and when the mixture begins to bubble, reduce the heat to low. Cover and simmer gently, stirring occasionally, for about 1 hour, until the meat is tender.

Stir in the rice, raisins, and chocolate, and continue cooking, stirring occasionally, for about 30 minutes, until the rice is tender.

Ladle into warmed bowls and garnish with cilantro.

SERVES 4

3 tbsp olive oil

1 lb 2 oz/500 g boneless braising beef, cut into 1-inch/2.5-cm pieces

1 onion, finely chopped

1 green bell pepper, cored, seeded, and finely chopped

1 small fresh red chile, seeded and finely chopped

2 garlic cloves, finely chopped

1 carrot, finely chopped

$1/4$ tsp ground coriander

$1/4$ tsp ground cumin

$1/8$ tsp ground cinnamon

$1/4$ tsp dried oregano

1 bay leaf

grated rind of $1/2$ orange

14 oz/400 g can chopped tomatoes

5 cups beef stock

$2/3$ cup red wine

$1/4$ cup long-grain white rice

3 tbsp raisins

$1/2$ oz/15 g semisweet chocolate, melted

chopped fresh cilantro, to garnish

Hearty Winter Broth

Cut the meat into small pieces, removing as much fat as possible. Put into a large pan and cover with the water. Bring to a boil over medium heat and skim off any foam that forms.

Add the pearl barley, reduce the heat, and cook gently, covered, for 1 hour.

Add the prepared vegetables and season well with salt and pepper. Continue to cook for an additional hour. Remove from the heat and let cool slightly.

Remove the meat from the pan using a slotted spoon and strip the meat from the bones. Discard the bones and any fat or gristle. Put the meat back into the pan and let cool thoroughly, then cover and refrigerate overnight.

Scrape the solidified fat off the surface of the soup. Reheat, season to taste with salt and pepper, and serve piping hot, garnished with the parsley scattered over the top.

SERVES 6–8

1 lb 9 oz/700 g neck of lamb

$7^{1}/_{4}$ cups water

1 cup pearl barley, rinsed

2 onions, chopped

1 garlic clove, finely chopped

3 small turnips, cut into small dice

3 carrots, peeled and thinly sliced

2 celery stalks, sliced

2 leeks, sliced

salt and pepper

2 tbsp chopped fresh parsley, to garnish

Chorizo & Red Kidney Bean Soup

Heat the oil in a large pan. Add the garlic and onions and cook over medium heat, stirring, for 3 minutes, until slightly softened. Add the bell pepper and cook for another 3 minutes, stirring. In a bowl, mix the cornstarch with enough stock to make a smooth paste and stir it into the pan. Cook, stirring, for 2 minutes. Stir in the remaining stock, then add the potatoes and season with salt and pepper. Bring to a boil, then lower the heat and simmer for 25 minutes, until the vegetables are tender.

Add the chorizo, zucchini, and kidney beans to the pan. Cook for 10 minutes, then stir in the cream and cook for another 5 minutes. Remove from the heat and ladle into serving bowls. Serve with slices of fresh crusty bread.

SERVES 4

2 tbsp olive oil

2 garlic cloves, chopped

2 red onions, chopped

1 red bell pepper, seeded and chopped

2 tbsp cornstarch

4 cups vegetable stock

1 lb/450 g potatoes, peeled, halved, and sliced

salt and pepper

5$\frac{1}{2}$ oz/150 g Spanish chorizo sausage, sliced

2 zucchini, trimmed and sliced

7 oz/200 g canned red kidney beans, drained

$\frac{1}{2}$ cup heavy cream

slices of fresh crusty bread, to serve

Chicken Gumbo Soup

Heat the oil in a large, heavy-bottom saucepan over medium-low heat and stir in the flour. Cook for about 15 minutes, stirring occasionally, until the mixture is a rich golden brown.

Add the onion, green bell pepper, and celery and continue cooking for about 10 minutes, until the onion softens.

Slowly pour in the stock and bring to a boil, stirring well and scraping the bottom of the pan to mix in the flour. Remove the pan from the heat.

Add the tomatoes and garlic. Stir in the okra and rice and season to taste with salt and pepper. Reduce the heat, cover, and simmer for 20 minutes, or until the okra is tender.

Add the chicken and sausage and continue simmering for about 10 minutes. Taste and adjust the seasoning, if necessary, and ladle into warmed bowls to serve.

SERVES 4

2 tbsp olive oil

4 tbsp all-purpose flour

1 onion, finely chopped

1 small green bell pepper, cored, seeded, and finely chopped

1 celery stalk, finely chopped

5 cups chicken stock

14 oz/400 g canned chopped tomatoes in juice

3 garlic cloves, finely chopped or crushed

$4^{1}/_{2}$ oz/125 g okra, stems removed, cut into $^{1}/_{4}$-inch/5-mm thick slices

4 tbsp white rice

salt and pepper

7 oz/200 g cooked chicken, cubed

4 oz/115 g cooked garlic sausage, sliced or cubed

Turkey & Lentil Soup

Heat the oil in a large pan. Add the garlic and onion and cook over medium heat, stirring, for 3 minutes, until slightly softened. Add the mushrooms, bell pepper, and tomatoes, and cook for another 5 minutes, stirring. Pour in the stock and red wine, then add the cauliflower, carrot, and red lentils. Season to taste with salt and pepper. Bring to a boil, then lower the heat and simmer for 25 minutes, until the vegetables are tender and cooked through.

Add the turkey and zucchini to the pan and cook for 10 minutes. Stir in the shredded basil and cook for another 5 minutes, then remove from the heat and ladle into serving bowls. Garnish with fresh basil leaves and serve with slices of fresh crusty bread.

SERVES 4

1 tbsp olive oil

1 garlic clove, chopped

1 large onion, chopped

7 oz/200 g button mushrooms, sliced

1 red bell pepper, seeded and chopped

6 tomatoes, skinned, seeded, and chopped

4 cups chicken stock

$2/3$ cup red wine

3 oz/85 g cauliflower florets

1 carrot, peeled and chopped

1 cup red lentils, rinsed

salt and pepper

12 oz/350 g cooked turkey meat, chopped

1 zucchini, trimmed and chopped

1 tbsp shredded fresh basil

fresh basil leaves, to garnish

thick slices of fresh crusty bread, to serve

Clam & Corn Chowder

Melt the butter in a large saucepan over medium-low heat. Add the onion and carrot and cook for 3–4 minutes, stirring frequently, until the onion is softened. Stir in the flour and continue cooking for 2 minutes.

Slowly add about half the stock and stir well, scraping the bottom of the pan to mix in the flour. Pour in the remaining stock and the water and bring just to a boil, stirring.

Add the potatoes, corn, and milk and stir to combine. Reduce the heat and simmer gently, partially covered, for about 20 minutes, stirring occasionally, until all the vegetables are tender.

Chop the clams, if large. Stir in the clams and continue cooking for about 5 minutes, until heated through. Taste and adjust the seasoning, if needed.

Ladle the soup into bowls and sprinkle with parsley.

SERVES 4

4 tsp butter

1 large onion, finely chopped

1 small carrot, finely diced

3 tbsp all-purpose flour

$1^{1}/_{4}$ cups fish stock

$^{3}/_{4}$ cup water

1 lb/450 g potatoes, diced

1 cup cooked or defrosted frozen corn

2 cups whole milk

10 oz/280 g canned clams, drained and rinsed

salt and pepper

chopped fresh parsley, to garnish

Meat Feasts

This chapter features slow-cooked, succulent stews and casseroles that simply melt deliciously in the mouth, whether beef, lamb, or pork. They have the additional benefit of being extremely economical because they use the less expensive cuts of meat. However, quicker-cooked but just as tasty dishes, such as a Sausage & Bean Casserole, are also included—perfect for a midweek supper.

Beef in Beer with Herb Dumplings

Preheat the oven to 325°F/160°C. Heat the oil in a flameproof casserole. Add the onions and carrots and cook over low heat, stirring occasionally, for 5 minutes, or until the onions are softened. Meanwhile, place the flour in a plastic bag and season with salt and pepper. Add the braising beef to the bag, tie the top, and shake well to coat. Do this in batches, if necessary.

Remove the vegetables from the casserole with a slotted spoon and reserve. Add the braising beef to the casserole, in batches, and cook, stirring frequently, until browned all over. Return all the meat and the onions and carrots to the casserole and sprinkle in any remaining seasoned flour. Pour in the stout and add the sugar, bay leaves, and thyme. Bring to a boil, cover, and transfer to the preheated oven to bake for 1¾ hours.

To make the herb dumplings, sift the flour and salt into a bowl. Stir in the suet and parsley and add enough of the water to make a soft dough. Shape into small balls between the palms of your hands. Add to the casserole and return to the oven for 30 minutes. Remove and discard the bay leaves and serve, sprinkled with parsley.

SERVES 6

2 tbsp corn oil

2 large onions, thinly sliced

8 carrots, sliced

4 tbsp all-purpose flour

salt and pepper

2 lb 12 oz/1.25 kg braising beef, cut into cubes

$1^3/_4$ cups stout beer

2 tsp brown sugar

2 bay leaves

1 tbsp chopped fresh thyme

herb dumplings

$3/_4$ cup self-rising flour

pinch of salt

$1/_2$ cup shredded suet

2 tbsp chopped fresh parsley, plus extra to garnish

about 4 tbsp water

Rich Beef Stew

Combine the wine, brandy, vinegar, shallots, carrots, garlic, peppercorns, thyme, rosemary, parsley, and bay leaf and season to taste with salt. Add the beef, stirring to coat, then cover with plastic wrap and let marinate in the refrigerator for 8 hours, or overnight.

Preheat the oven to 300°F/150°C. Drain the beef, reserving the marinade, and pat dry on paper towels. Heat half the oil in a large, flameproof casserole. Add the beef cubes in batches and cook over medium heat, stirring, for 3–4 minutes, or until browned. Transfer the beef to a plate with a slotted spoon. Brown the remaining beef, adding more oil, if necessary.

Return all of the beef to the casserole and add the tomatoes and their juices, mushrooms, and orange rind. Strain the reserved marinade into the casserole. Bring to a boil, cover, and cook in the oven for 2½ hours.

Remove the casserole from the oven, add the prosciutto and olives, and return it to the oven to cook for an additional 30 minutes, or until the beef is very tender. Discard the orange rind and serve straight from the casserole, garnished with parsley.

SERVES 6

1¹/₂ cups dry white wine

2 tbsp brandy

1 tbsp white wine vinegar

4 shallots, sliced

4 carrots, sliced

1 garlic clove, finely chopped

6 black peppercorns

4 fresh thyme sprigs

1 fresh rosemary sprig

2 fresh parsley sprigs, plus extra
 to garnish

1 bay leaf

salt

1 lb 10 oz/750 g beef top round,
 cut into 1-inch/2.5-cm cubes

2 tbsp olive oil

1 lb 12 oz/800 g canned chopped
 tomatoes

8 oz/225 g portobello mushrooms,
 sliced

strip of finely pared orange rind

2 oz/55 g prosciutto, cut into strips

12 black olives

Beef Goulash

Heat the vegetable oil in a large pan and cook the onion and garlic for 3–4 minutes.

Cut the braising beef into chunks and cook over high heat for 3 minutes until browned all over. Add the paprika and stir well, then add the chopped tomatoes, tomato paste, bell pepper, and mushrooms. Cook for 2 minutes, stirring frequently.

Pour in the beef stock. Bring to a boil, then reduce the heat. Cover and simmer for 1½–2 hours, until the meat is tender.

Blend the cornstarch with the water, then add to the pan, stirring until thickened and smooth. Cook for 1 minute, then season with salt and pepper to taste.

Put the yogurt in a serving bowl and sprinkle with a little paprika.

Transfer the beef goulash to a warmed serving dish, garnish with chopped fresh parsley, and serve with rice and yogurt.

SERVES 4

2 tbsp vegetable oil

1 large onion, chopped

1 garlic clove, crushed

1 lb 10 oz/750 g lean braising beef

2 tbsp paprika

15 oz/425 g canned chopped tomatoes

2 tbsp tomato paste

1 large red bell pepper, seeded and chopped

6 oz/175 g button mushrooms, sliced

2½ cups beef stock

1 tbsp cornstarch

1 tbsp water

salt and pepper

4 tbsp low-fat plain yogurt

paprika, for sprinkling

chopped fresh parsley, to garnish

freshly cooked long-grain and wild rice, to serve

Lamb & Potato Stew

Preheat the oven to 325°F/160°C. Spread the flour on a plate and season with salt and pepper. Roll the pieces of lamb in the flour to coat, shaking off any excess, and arrange in the bottom of a casserole.

Layer the onions, carrots, and potatoes on top of the lamb.

Sprinkle in the thyme and pour in the stock, then cover and cook in the preheated oven for 2^1/$_2$ hours. Garnish with the chopped parsley and serve straight from the casserole.

SERVES 4

4 tbsp all-purpose flour

salt and pepper

3 lb/1.3 kg middle neck of lamb, trimmed of visible fat

3 large onions, chopped

3 carrots, sliced

1 lb/450 g potatoes, cut into quarters

^{1}/$_2$ tsp dried thyme

3^1/$_2$ cups hot beef stock

2 tbsp chopped fresh parsley, to garnish

Lamb Stew with Chickpeas

Heat 4 tablespoons of the oil in a large, heavy-bottom flameproof casserole over medium-high heat. Reduce the heat, add the chorizo, and cook for 1 minute. Transfer to a plate. Add the onions to the casserole and cook for 2 minutes, then add the garlic and continue cooking for 3 minutes, or until the onions are soft but not brown. Remove from the casserole and set aside.

Heat the remaining 2 tablespoons of oil in the casserole. Add the lamb cubes in a single layer without overcrowding the casserole, and cook until browned on each side; work in batches, if necessary.

Return the onion mixture and chorizo to the casserole with all the lamb. Stir in the stock, wine, vinegar, tomatoes with their juices, and salt and pepper to taste. Bring to a boil, scraping any glazed bits from the bottom of the casserole. Reduce the heat and stir in the thyme, bay leaves, and paprika.

Transfer to a preheated oven set to 325°F/160°C, and cook, covered, for 40–45 minutes, until the lamb is tender. Stir in the chickpeas and return to the oven, uncovered, for 10 minutes, or until they are heated through and the juices are reduced.

Taste and adjust the seasoning. Garnish with thyme and serve.

SERVES 4–6

6 tbsp olive oil

8 oz/225 g Spanish chorizo sausage, cut into $^1/_4$-inch/5-mm thick slices, casings removed

2 large onions, chopped

6 large garlic cloves, crushed

2 lb/900 g boned leg of lamb, cut into 2-inch/5-cm cubes

$1^1/_4$ cups lamb stock or water

$^1/_2$ cup red wine, such as Rioja or Tempranillo

2 tbsp sherry vinegar

1 lb 12 oz/800 g canned chopped tomatoes

salt and pepper

4 sprigs fresh thyme

2 bay leaves

$^1/_2$ tsp sweet Spanish paprika

1 lb 12 oz/800 g canned chickpeas, rinsed and drained

sprigs of fresh thyme, to garnish

Lamb with Pears

Preheat the oven to 325°F/160°C. Heat the olive oil in a flameproof casserole over medium heat. Add the lamb and cook, turning frequently, for 5–10 minutes, or until browned on all sides.

Arrange the pear pieces on top, then sprinkle over the ginger. Cover with the potatoes. Pour in the cider and season to taste with salt and pepper. Cover and cook in the preheated oven for 1¼ hours.

Trim the stem ends of the green beans. Remove the casserole from the oven and add the beans, then re-cover and return to the oven for an additional 30 minutes. Taste and adjust the seasoning and sprinkle with the chives. Serve immediately.

SERVES 4

1 tbsp olive oil

2 lb 4 oz/1 kg best end-of-neck lamb
   cutlets, trimmed of visible fat

6 pears, peeled, cored, and cut
   into quarters

1 tsp ground ginger

4 potatoes, diced

4 tbsp hard cider

salt and pepper

1 lb/450 g green beans

2 tbsp snipped fresh chives,
   to garnish

Pork & Vegetable Stew

Trim off any fat or gristle from the pork and cut into thin strips about 2 inches/5 cm long. Mix the flour and spices together. Toss the pork in the spiced flour until well coated and reserve any remaining spiced flour.

Heat the oil in a large, heavy-bottom pan and cook the onion, stirring frequently, for 5 minutes, or until softened. Add the pork and cook over high heat, stirring frequently, for 5 minutes, or until browned on all sides and sealed. Sprinkle in the reserved spiced flour and cook, stirring constantly, for 2 minutes, then remove from the heat.

Gradually add the tomatoes to the pan. Blend the tomato paste with a little of the stock in a pitcher or small bowl and gradually stir into the pan, then stir in half the remaining stock.

Add the carrots, then return to the heat and bring to a boil, stirring. Reduce the heat, then cover and simmer, stirring occasionally, for 1 1/2 hours. Add the squash and cook for an additional 15 minutes.

Add the leeks and okra, and the remaining stock if you prefer a thinner stew. Simmer for an additional 15 minutes, or until the pork and vegetables are tender. Season to taste with salt and pepper, then garnish with fresh parsley and serve with couscous.

SERVES 4

1 lb/450 g lean boneless pork

1 1/2 tbsp all-purpose flour

1 tsp ground coriander

1 tsp ground cumin

1 1/2 tsp ground cinnamon

1 tbsp olive oil

1 onion, chopped

14 oz/400 g canned chopped
   tomatoes

2 tbsp tomato paste

1 1/4–2 cups chicken stock

8 oz/225 g carrots, chopped

12 oz/350 g squash, such as
   kabocha, peeled, seeded, and
   chopped

8 oz/225 g leeks, sliced, blanched,
   and drained

4 oz/115 g okra, trimmed and sliced

salt and pepper

sprigs of fresh parsley, to garnish

couscous, to serve

Sausage & Bean Casserole

Prick the sausages all over with a fork. Heat 2 tablespoons of the oil in a large, heavy skillet. Add the sausages and cook over low heat, turning frequently, for 10–15 minutes, until evenly browned and cooked through. Remove them from the skillet and keep warm. Drain off the oil and wipe out the skillet with paper towels.

Heat the remaining oil in the skillet. Add the onion, garlic, and bell pepper to the skillet and cook for 5 minutes, stirring occasionally, or until softened.

Add the tomatoes to the skillet and let the mixture simmer for about 5 minutes, stirring occasionally, or until slightly reduced and thickened.

Stir the sun-dried tomato paste, cannellini beans, and Italian sausages into the mixture in the skillet. Cook for 4–5 minutes or until the mixture is piping hot. Add 4–5 tablespoons of water if the mixture becomes too dry during cooking.

Transfer the Italian sausage and bean casserole to serving plates and serve with mashed potatoes or cooked rice.

SERVES 4

8 Italian sausages

3 tbsp olive oil

1 large onion, chopped

2 garlic cloves, chopped

1 green bell pepper, seeded and sliced

8 oz/225 g fresh tomatoes, skinned and chopped or 14 oz/400 g canned chopped tomatoes

2 tbsp sun-dried tomato paste

14 oz/400 g canned cannellini beans

mashed potatoes or rice, to serve

Pot-roast Pork

Heat the oil with half the butter in a heavy-bottom pan or flameproof casserole. Add the pork and cook over medium heat, turning frequently, for 5–10 minutes, or until browned. Transfer to a plate.

Add the shallots to the pan and cook, stirring frequently, for 5 minutes, or until softened. Add the juniper berries and thyme sprigs and return the pork to the pan, with any juices that have collected on the plate. Pour in the cider and stock, season to taste with salt and pepper, then cover and simmer for 30 minutes. Turn the pork over and add the celery. Re-cover the pan and cook for an additional 40 minutes.

Meanwhile, make a beurre manié by mashing the remaining butter with the flour in a small bowl. Transfer the pork and celery to a platter with a slotted spoon and keep warm. Remove and discard the juniper berries and thyme. Whisk the beurre manié, a little at a time, into the simmering cooking liquid. Cook, stirring constantly, for 2 minutes, then stir in the cream and bring to a boil.

Slice the pork and spoon a little of the sauce over it. Garnish with thyme sprigs and serve immediately with the celery, peas, and remaining sauce.

SERVES 4

1 tbsp corn oil

$1/4$ cup butter

2 lb 4 oz/1 kg boned and rolled pork loin

4 shallots, chopped

6 juniper berries

2 fresh thyme sprigs, plus extra to garnish

$2/3$ cup hard cider

$2/3$ cup chicken stock or water

salt and pepper

8 celery stalks, chopped

2 tbsp all-purpose flour

$2/3$ cup heavy cream

freshly cooked peas, to serve

3

Poultry Pot Wonders

One-pot cooking is the perfect technique for poultry, especially chicken, which can sometimes be disappointingly bland and dry when cooked in other ways. Fabulous stews and delicious casseroles burst with flavor and vitality. Discover the versatility of poultry with these inspiring international recipes for chicken, turkey, and duck.

Coq au Vin

Melt half the butter with the olive oil in a large, flameproof casserole. Add the chicken and cook over medium heat, stirring, for 8–10 minutes, or until golden brown. Add the bacon, onions, mushrooms, and garlic.

Pour in the brandy and set it alight with a match or taper. When the flames have died down, add the wine, stock, and bouquet garni and season to taste with salt and pepper. Bring to a boil, reduce the heat, and simmer gently for 1 hour, or until the chicken pieces are cooked through and tender. Meanwhile, make a beurre manié by mashing the remaining butter with the flour in a small bowl.

Remove and discard the bouquet garni. Transfer the chicken to a large plate and keep warm. Stir the beurre manié into the casserole, a little at a time. Bring to a boil, return the chicken to the casserole, and serve immediately, garnished with bay leaves.

SERVES 4

$^1/_4$ cup butter

2 tbsp olive oil

4 lb / 1.8 kg chicken pieces

4 oz / 115 g rindless smoked bacon, cut into strips

4 oz / 115 g pearl onions, peeled

4 oz / 115 g cremini mushrooms, halved

2 garlic cloves, finely chopped

2 tbsp brandy

1 cup red wine

$1^1/_4$ cups chicken stock

1 bouquet garni

salt and pepper

2 tbsp all-purpose flour

bay leaves, to garnish

Brunswick Stew

Season the chicken pieces with salt and dust with paprika.

Heat the oil and butter in a flameproof casserole or large pan. Add the chicken pieces and cook over medium heat, turning, for 10–15 minutes, or until golden. Transfer to a plate with a slotted spoon.

Add the onions and bell peppers to the casserole. Cook over low heat, stirring occasionally, for 5 minutes, or until softened. Add the tomatoes, wine, stock, Worcestershire sauce, Tabasco sauce, and parsley and bring to a boil, stirring. Return the chicken to the casserole, cover, and simmer, stirring occasionally, for 30 minutes.

Add the corn and beans to the casserole, partially re-cover, and simmer for an additional 30 minutes. Place the flour and water in a small bowl and mix to make a paste. Stir a ladleful of the cooking liquid into the paste, then stir it into the stew. Cook, stirring frequently, for 5 minutes. Serve, garnished with parsley.

SERVES 6

4 lb / 1.8 kg chicken pieces

salt

2 tbsp paprika

2 tbsp olive oil

2 tbsp butter

1 lb / 450 g onions, chopped

2 yellow bell peppers, seeded and chopped

14 oz / 400 g canned chopped tomatoes

1 cup dry white wine

1^3/$_4$ cups chicken stock

1 tbsp Worcestershire sauce

^{1}/$_2$ tsp Tabasco sauce

1 tbsp finely chopped fresh parsley

11^1/$_2$ oz / 325 g canned corn kernels, drained

15 oz / 425 g canned lima beans, drained and rinsed

2 tbsp all-purpose flour

4 tbsp water

chopped fresh parsley, to garnish

Chicken Tagine

Heat the oil in a large pan over medium heat, add the onion and garlic, and cook for 3 minutes, stirring frequently. Add the chicken and cook, stirring constantly, for an additional 5 minutes, or until sealed on all sides. Add the cumin and cinnamon sticks to the pan halfway through sealing the chicken.

Sprinkle in the flour and cook, stirring constantly, for 2 minutes.

Add the eggplant, red bell pepper, and mushrooms and cook for an additional 2 minutes, stirring constantly.

Blend the tomato paste with the stock, stir into the pan, and bring to a boil. Reduce the heat and add the chickpeas and apricots. Cover and let simmer for 15–20 minutes, or until the chicken is tender.

Season with salt and pepper to taste and serve at once, sprinkled with cilantro.

SERVES 4

1 tbsp olive oil

1 onion, cut into small wedges

2–4 garlic cloves, sliced

1 lb/450 g skinless, boneless chicken breast, diced

1 tsp ground cumin

2 cinnamon sticks, lightly bruised

1 tbsp whole-wheat flour

8 oz/225 g eggplant, diced

1 red bell pepper, seeded and chopped

3 oz/85 g button mushrooms, sliced

1 tbsp tomato paste

$2^{1}/_{2}$ cups chicken stock

10 oz/280 g canned chickpeas, drained and rinsed

$^{1}/_{3}$ cup chopped no-soak apricots

salt and pepper

1 tbsp chopped fresh cilantro

Chicken in White Wine

Preheat the oven to 325°F/160°C. Melt half the butter with the oil in a flameproof casserole. Add the bacon and cook over medium heat, stirring, for 5–10 minutes, or until golden brown. Transfer the bacon to a large plate. Add the onions and garlic to the casserole and cook over low heat, stirring occasionally, for 10 minutes, or until golden. Transfer to the plate. Add the chicken and cook over medium heat, stirring constantly, for 8–10 minutes, or until golden. Transfer to the plate.

Drain off any excess fat from the casserole. Stir in the wine and stock and bring to a boil, scraping any sediment off the bottom. Add the bouquet garni and season to taste. Return the bacon, onions, and chicken to the casserole. Cover and cook in the preheated oven for 1 hour. Add the mushrooms, re-cover, and cook for 15 minutes. Meanwhile, make a beurre manié by mashing the remaining butter with the flour in a small bowl.

Remove the casserole from the oven and set over medium heat. Remove and discard the bouquet garni. Whisk in the beurre manié, a little at a time. Bring to a boil, stirring constantly, then serve, garnished with fresh herb sprigs.

SERVES 4

$^1/_4$ cup butter

2 tbsp olive oil

2 thick, rindless, lean bacon strips, chopped

4 oz/115 g pearl onions, peeled

1 garlic clove, finely chopped

4 lb/1.8 kg chicken pieces

$1^3/_4$ cups dry white wine

$1^1/_4$ cups chicken stock

1 bouquet garni

salt and pepper

4 oz/115 g button mushrooms

$2^1/_2$ tbsp all-purpose flour

fresh herb sprigs, to garnish

Louisiana Chicken

Heat the oil in a large, heavy-bottom pan or flameproof casserole. Add the chicken and cook over medium heat, stirring, for 5–10 minutes, or until golden. Transfer the chicken to a plate with a slotted spoon.

Stir the flour into the oil and cook over very low heat, stirring constantly, for 15 minutes, or until light golden. Do not let it burn. Immediately, add the onion, celery, and green bell pepper and cook, stirring constantly, for 2 minutes. Add the garlic, thyme, and chiles and cook, stirring, for 1 minute.

Stir in the tomatoes and their juices, then gradually stir in the stock. Return the chicken pieces to the pan, cover, and simmer for 45 minutes, or until the chicken is cooked through and tender. Season to taste with salt and pepper, transfer to warmed serving plates, and serve immediately, garnished with some corn salad and a sprinkling of chopped thyme.

SERVES 4

5 tbsp corn oil

4 chicken portions

6 tbsp all-purpose flour

1 onion, chopped

2 celery stalks, sliced

1 green bell pepper, seeded and chopped

2 garlic cloves, finely chopped

2 tsp chopped fresh thyme

2 fresh red chiles, seeded and finely chopped

14 oz/400 g canned chopped tomatoes

$1^1/_4$ cups chicken stock

salt and pepper

to garnish

corn salad

chopped fresh thyme

Chicken with Garlic

Sift the flour onto a large plate and season with paprika and salt and pepper to taste. Dredge the chicken pieces with the flour on both sides, shaking off the excess.

Heat 4 tablespoons of the oil in a large, deep skillet or flameproof casserole over medium heat. Add the garlic and cook, stirring frequently, for about 2 minutes to flavor the oil. Remove with a slotted spoon and set aside to drain on paper towels.

Add as many chicken pieces, skin-side down, as will fit in a single layer. (Work in batches to avoid overcrowding the skillet, adding a little extra oil if necessary.) Cook for 5 minutes, until the skin is golden brown. Turn over and cook for 5 minutes longer.

Pour off any excess oil. Return the garlic and chicken pieces to the skillet and add the chicken stock, wine, and herbs. Bring to a boil, then reduce the heat, cover, and let simmer for 20–25 minutes, until the chicken is cooked through and tender and the garlic is very soft.

Transfer the chicken pieces to a serving platter and keep warm. Bring the cooking liquid to a boil, with the garlic and herbs, and boil until reduced to about 1½ cups. Remove and discard the herbs. Taste and adjust the seasoning, if necessary.

Spoon the sauce and the garlic cloves over the chicken pieces. Garnish with the parsley and thyme, and serve.

SERVES 4

4 tbsp all-purpose flour

Spanish paprika, either hot or smoked sweet, to taste

salt and pepper

1 large chicken, about 3 lb 12 oz/ 1.75 kg, cut into 8 pieces, rinsed, and patted dry

4–6 tbsp olive oil

24 large garlic cloves, peeled and halved

2 cups chicken stock, preferably homemade

4 tbsp dry white wine, such as white Rioja

2 sprigs of fresh parsley, 1 bay leaf, and 1 sprig of fresh thyme, tied together

fresh parsley and thyme leaves, to garnish

Italian Turkey Steaks

Heat the oil in a flameproof casserole or heavy-bottom skillet. Add the turkey steaks and cook over medium heat for 5–10 minutes, turning occasionally, until golden. Transfer to a plate.

Seed and slice the red bell peppers. Slice the onion, add to the skillet with the bell peppers, and cook over low heat, stirring occasionally, for 5 minutes, or until softened. Add the garlic and cook for an additional 2 minutes. Return the turkey to the skillet and add the strained tomatoes, wine, and marjoram. Season to taste. Bring to a boil, then reduce the heat, cover, and simmer, stirring occasionally, for 25–30 minutes, or until the turkey is cooked through and tender.

Stir in the cannellini beans. Simmer for an additional 5 minutes. Sprinkle the bread crumbs over the top and place under a preheated medium-hot broiler for 2–3 minutes, or until golden. Serve, garnished with basil, if using.

SERVES 4

1 tbsp olive oil

4 turkey steaks or scallops

2 red bell peppers

1 red onion

2 garlic cloves, finely chopped

1$^1/_4$ cups strained tomatoes

$^2/_3$ cup medium white wine

1 tbsp chopped fresh marjoram

salt and pepper

14 oz/400 g canned cannellini
    beans, drained and rinsed

3 tbsp fresh white breadcrumbs

fresh basil sprigs, to garnish
    (optional)

Duck Legs with Olives

Put the duck legs in the bottom of a flameproof casserole or a large, heavy-bottom skillet with a tight-fitting lid. Add the tomatoes, garlic, onion, carrot, celery, thyme, and olives, and stir together. Season with salt and pepper to taste.

Turn the heat to high and cook, uncovered, until the ingredients start to bubble. Reduce the heat to low, cover tightly, and let simmer for 1¼–1½ hours, until the duck is very tender. Check occasionally and add a little water if the mixture appears to be drying out.

When the duck is tender, transfer it to a serving platter, cover, and keep hot in a preheated warm oven. Leave the casserole uncovered, increase the heat to medium, and cook, stirring, for about 10 minutes, until the mixture forms a sauce. Stir in the orange rind, then taste and adjust the seasoning if necessary.

Mash the tender garlic cloves with a fork and spread over the duck legs. Spoon the sauce over the top. Serve at once.

SERVES 4

4 duck legs, all visible fat trimmed off

1 lb 12 oz/800 g canned tomatoes, chopped

8 garlic cloves, peeled, but left whole

1 large onion, chopped

1 carrot, finely chopped

1 celery stalk, finely chopped

3 sprigs fresh thyme

½ cup Spanish green olives in brine, stuffed with pimientos, garlic, or almonds, drained and rinsed

salt and pepper

1 tsp finely grated orange rind

Fish & Seafood Suppers

From fiery fish dishes to hearty stews, these dishes prove once and for all that cooking—and eating—fish is not a chore, but a pleasure. For many of us, fish and seafood, with its light fresh taste, may be something we only eat on our summer vacations. However, these recipes demonstrate how well it takes on more robust flavors, making it perfect for winter dishes, too. Classic fish and seafood dishes are the perfect choice for impressive entertaining and the quicker cooking time also makes for speedy suppers.

Seafood Stew

Put the saffron threads in a heatproof pitcher or small bowl with the water and let stand for at least 10 minutes to infuse.

Heat the oil in a large, heavy-bottom flameproof casserole over medium-high heat. Reduce the heat to low and cook the onion, stirring occasionally, for 10 minutes, or until golden but not browned. Stir in the garlic, thyme, bay leaves, and red bell peppers and cook, stirring frequently, for 5 minutes, or until the bell peppers are softened and the onions have softened further. Add the tomatoes and paprika and simmer, stirring frequently, for an additional 5 minutes.

Stir in the stock, the saffron and its soaking liquid, and the almonds and bring to a boil, stirring. Reduce the heat and simmer for 5–10 minutes, or until the sauce reduces and thickens. Season to taste with salt and pepper.

Meanwhile, clean the mussels and clams by scrubbing or scraping the shells and pulling out any beards that are attached to the mussels. Discard any with broken shells or any that refuse to close when tapped.

Gently stir the hake into the stew so that it doesn't break up, then add the shrimp, mussels, and clams. Reduce the heat to very low, then cover and simmer for 5 minutes, or until the hake is opaque, the mussels and clams have opened, and the shrimp have turned pink. Discard any mussels or clams that remain closed. Serve immediately with plenty of thick crusty bread for soaking up the juices.

SERVES 4–6

large pinch of saffron threads

4 tbsp almost boiling water

6 tbsp olive oil

1 large onion, chopped

2 garlic cloves, finely chopped

1½ tbsp chopped fresh thyme leaves

2 bay leaves

2 red bell peppers, seeded and coarsely chopped

1 lb 12 oz/800 g canned chopped tomatoes

1 tsp smoked paprika

1 cup fish stock

1 cup blanched almonds, toasted and finely ground

salt and pepper

12–16 live mussels

12–16 live clams

1 lb 5 oz/600 g thick boned hake or cod fillets, skinned and cut into 2-inch/5-cm chunks

12–16 raw shrimp, shelled and deveined

thick crusty bread, to serve

Seafood Risotto

Heat the oil with 2 tablespoons of the butter in a deep pan over medium heat until the butter has melted. Add the garlic and cook, stirring, for 1 minute.

Reduce the heat, add the rice, and mix to coat in oil and butter. Cook, stirring constantly, for 2–3 minutes, or until the grains are translucent.

Gradually add the hot stock, a ladleful at a time. Stir constantly and add more liquid as the rice absorbs each addition. Increase the heat to medium so that the liquid bubbles. Cook for 20 minutes, or until all the liquid is absorbed and the rice is creamy. About 5 minutes before the rice is ready, add the seafood and oregano to the pan and mix well.

Remove the pan from the heat and season to taste. Add the remaining butter and mix well, then stir in the grated cheese until it melts. Spoon onto warmed plates and serve at once, garnished with extra oregano.

SERVES 4

1 tbsp olive oil

2 oz/55 g butter

2 garlic cloves, chopped

$1^3/_4$ cups risotto rice

$5^1/_2$ cups boiling fish or chicken stock

9 oz/250 g mixed cooked seafood, such as shrimp, squid, mussels, and clams

2 tbsp chopped fresh oregano, plus extra to garnish

salt and pepper

$^1/_2$ cup freshly grated romano or Parmesan cheese

Seafood in Saffron Sauce

Clean the mussels and clams by scrubbing or scraping the shells and pulling out any beards that are attached to the mussels. Discard any with broken shells or any that refuse to close when tapped.

Heat the oil in a large, flameproof casserole and cook the onion with the saffron, thyme, and a pinch of salt over low heat, stirring occasionally, for 5 minutes, or until softened.

Add the garlic and cook, stirring, for 2 minutes. Add the tomatoes, wine, and stock, then season to taste with salt and pepper and stir well. Bring to a boil, then reduce the heat and simmer for 15 minutes.

Add the fish chunks and simmer for an additional 3 minutes. Add the clams, mussels, and squid rings and simmer for an additional 5 minutes, or until the mussels and clams have opened. Discard any that remain closed. Stir in the basil and serve immediately, accompanied by plenty of fresh bread to mop up the broth.

SERVES 4

8 oz/225 g live mussels

8 oz/225 g live clams

2 tbsp olive oil

1 onion, sliced

pinch of saffron threads

1 tbsp chopped fresh thyme

salt and pepper

2 garlic cloves, finely chopped

1 lb 12 oz/800 g canned tomatoes, drained and chopped

$^3/_4$ cup dry white wine

8 cups fish stock

12 oz/350 g red snapper fillets, cut into bite-size chunks

1 lb/450 g monkfish fillet, cut into bite-size chunks

8 oz/225 g raw squid rings

2 tbsp fresh shredded basil leaves

fresh bread, to serve

Shellfish Chili

Place the shrimp, scallops, monkfish chunks, and lime slices in a large, nonmetallic dish with ¼ teaspoon of the chili powder, ¼ teaspoon of the ground cumin, 1 tablespoon of the chopped cilantro, half the garlic, the fresh chile, and 1 tablespoon of the oil. Cover with plastic wrap and let marinate for up to 1 hour.

Meanwhile, heat 1 tablespoon of the remaining oil in a flameproof casserole or large, heavy-bottom pan. Add the onion, the remaining garlic, and the red and yellow bell peppers and cook over low heat, stirring occasionally, for 5 minutes, or until softened. Add the remaining chili powder, the remaining cumin, the cloves, cinnamon, and cayenne with the remaining oil, if necessary, and season to taste with salt. Cook, stirring, for 5 minutes, then gradually stir in the stock and the tomatoes and their juices. Partially cover and simmer for 25 minutes.

Add the beans to the tomato mixture and spoon the fish and shellfish on top. Cover and cook for 10 minutes, or until the fish and shellfish are cooked through. Sprinkle with the remaining cilantro and serve.

SERVES 4

4 oz/115 g raw shrimp, peeled

9 oz/250 g prepared scallops, thawed if frozen

4 oz/115 g monkfish fillet, cut into chunks

1 lime, peeled and thinly sliced

1 tbsp chili powder

1 tsp ground cumin

3 tbsp chopped fresh cilantro

2 garlic cloves, finely chopped

1 fresh green chile, seeded and chopped

3 tbsp corn oil

1 onion, coarsely chopped

1 red bell pepper, seeded and coarsely chopped

1 yellow bell pepper, seeded and coarsely chopped

¼ tsp ground cloves

pinch of ground cinnamon

pinch of cayenne pepper

salt

1½ cups fish stock

14 oz/400 g canned chopped tomatoes

14 oz/400 g canned red kidney beans, drained and rinsed

Shrimp with Coconut Rice

Place the mushrooms in a small bowl, cover with hot water, and set aside to soak for 30 minutes. Drain, then cut off and discard the stalks and slice the caps.

Heat 1 tablespoon of the oil in a wok and stir-fry the scallions, coconut, and chile for 2–3 minutes, until lightly browned. Add the mushrooms and stir-fry for 3–4 minutes.

Add the rice and stir-fry for 2–3 minutes, then add the stock and bring to a boil. Reduce the heat and add the coconut milk. Let simmer for 10–15 minutes, until the rice is tender. Stir in the shrimp and basil, heat through, and serve.

SERVES 4

1 cup dried Chinese mushrooms

2 tbsp vegetable or peanut oil

6 scallions, chopped

$^1/_2$ cup dry unsweetened coconut

1 fresh green chile, seeded and
   chopped

1 cup jasmine rice

$^2/_3$ cup fish stock

$1^3/_4$ cups coconut milk

12 oz/350 g cooked shelled shrimp

6 sprigs fresh Thai basil

Spicy Monkfish Rice

In a food processor or blender, blend the fresh and dried chile, garlic, saffron, mint, olive oil, and lemon juice until finely chopped but not smooth.

Put the monkfish into a nonmetallic dish and pour over the spice paste, mixing together well. Set aside for 20 minutes to marinate.

Heat a large pan until it is very hot. Using a slotted spoon, lift the monkfish from the marinade and add, in batches, to the hot pan. Cook for 3–4 minutes, until browned and firm. Remove with a slotted spoon and set aside while you cook the rice.

Add the onion and remaining marinade to the same pan and cook for 5 minutes, until softened and lightly browned. Add the rice and stir until well coated. Add the tomatoes and coconut milk. Bring to a boil, cover, and simmer very gently for 15 minutes. Stir in the peas, season, and arrange the fish over the top. Cover with foil and continue to cook over very low heat for 5 minutes. Serve garnished with the chopped mint.

SERVES 4

1 hot red chile, seeded and chopped

1 tsp chile flakes

2 garlic cloves, chopped

2 pinches of saffron

3 tbsp coarsely chopped mint leaves

4 tbsp olive oil

2 tbsp lemon juice

12 oz/350 g monkfish fillet, cut into bite-sized pieces

1 onion, finely chopped

1 cup long-grain rice

14 oz/400 g canned chopped tomatoes

$^3/_4$ cup coconut milk

1 cup peas

salt and pepper

2 tbsp chopped fresh mint, to garnish

Shrimp & Chicken Paella

Soak the mussels in lightly salted water for 10 minutes. Put the saffron threads and water in a small bowl or cup and let infuse for a few minutes. Meanwhile, put the rice in a strainer and rinse in cold water until the water runs clear. Set aside.

Clean the mussels by scrubbing the shells and pulling out any beards that are attached to them. Discard any with broken shells or any that refuse to close when tapped. Set aside.

Heat 3 tablespoons of the oil in a 12-inch/30-cm paella pan or ovenproof casserole. Cook the chicken thighs over medium-high heat, turning frequently, for 5 minutes, or until golden and crispy. Using a slotted spoon, transfer to a bowl. Add the chorizo to the pan and cook, stirring, for 1 minute, or until beginning to crisp. Add to the chicken.

Heat the remaining oil in the pan and cook the onions, stirring frequently, for 2 minutes, then add the garlic and paprika and cook for an additional 3 minutes, or until the onions are soft but not browned.

Add the drained rice, beans, and peas and stir until coated in oil. Return the chicken and chorizo and any accumulated juices to the pan. Stir in the stock, saffron and its soaking liquid, and salt and pepper to taste and bring to a boil, stirring constantly. Reduce the heat to low and let simmer, uncovered and without stirring, for 15 minutes, or until the rice is almost tender and most of the liquid has been absorbed.

Arrange the mussels, shrimp, and red bell peppers on top, then cover and simmer, without stirring, for an additional 5 minutes, or until the shrimp turn pink and the mussels open. Discard any mussels that remain closed. Taste and adjust the seasoning if necessary. Sprinkle with the parsley and serve immediately.

SERVES 6–8

16 live mussels

$1/2$ tsp saffron threads

2 tbsp hot water

$1^3/4$ cups medium-grain paella rice

6 tbsp olive oil

6–8 unboned, skin-on chicken thighs, excess fat removed

5 oz/140 g Spanish chorizo sausage, casing removed, cut into $1/4$-inch/5-mm slices

2 large onions, chopped

4 large garlic cloves, crushed

1 tsp mild or hot Spanish paprika, to taste

$3^1/2$ oz/100 g green beans, chopped

$3/4$ cup frozen peas

5 cups fish, chicken, or vegetable stock

salt and pepper

16 raw shrimp, shelled and deveined

2 red bell peppers, halved and seeded, then broiled, peeled, and sliced

$1^1/4$ oz/35 g fresh chopped parsley, to garnish

Vegetable Heaven

Eating plenty of healthy vegetables every day could not be easier or more fun than with this superb collection of international recipes. Whether your taste is for a hearty bean stew, an aromatic casserole, or a satisfying risotto, these delicious and easy-to-prepare vegetable dishes are sure to fill the bill. Economical, irresistible, nourishing, and all in a single pot—what more could anyone want?

Tuscan Bean Stew

Trim the fennel and reserve any feathery fronds, then cut the bulb into small strips. Heat the oil in a large, heavy-bottom pan with a tight-fitting lid, and cook the onion, garlic, chile, and fennel strips, stirring frequently, for 5–8 minutes, or until softened.

Add the eggplant and cook, stirring frequently, for 5 minutes. Blend the tomato paste with a little of the stock and pour over the fennel mixture, then add the remaining stock, and the tomatoes, vinegar, and oregano. Bring to a boil, then reduce the heat and simmer, covered, for 15 minutes, or until the tomatoes have begun to collapse.

Drain and rinse the beans, then drain again. Add them to the pan with the yellow bell pepper, zucchini, and olives. Simmer for an additional 15 minutes, or until the vegetables are tender. Taste and adjust the seasoning. Scatter with the Parmesan shavings and serve garnished with the reserved fennel fronds, accompanied by polenta wedges or crusty bread.

SERVES 4

1 large fennel bulb

2 tbsp olive oil

1 red onion, cut into small wedges

2–4 garlic cloves, sliced

1 fresh green chile, seeded
and chopped

1 small eggplant, about 8 oz/225 g,
cut into chunks

2 tbsp tomato paste

2–2$^{1}/_{2}$ cups vegetable stock

1 lb/450 g ripe tomatoes

1 tbsp balsamic vinegar

a few sprigs of fresh oregano

14 oz/400 g canned cranberry
beans

14 oz/400 g canned flageolets

1 yellow bell pepper, seeded and cut
into small strips

1 zucchini, sliced into semicircles

$^{1}/_{3}$ cup pitted black olives

salt and pepper

25 g/1 oz Parmesan cheese,
freshly shaved

polenta wedges or crusty bread,
to serve

Vegetable Goulash

Put the sun-dried tomatoes in a small heatproof bowl, then cover with almost boiling water and let soak for 15–20 minutes. Drain, reserving the soaking liquid.

Heat the oil in a large, heavy-bottom pan with a tight-fitting lid, and cook the chiles, garlic, and vegetables, stirring frequently, for 5–8 minutes, or until softened. Blend the tomato paste with a little of the stock and pour over the vegetable mixture, then add the remaining stock, lentils, the sun-dried tomatoes and their soaking liquid, and the paprika and thyme.

Bring to a boil, then reduce the heat and simmer, covered, for 15 minutes. Add the fresh tomatoes and simmer for an additional 15 minutes, or until the vegetables and lentils are tender. Serve topped with spoonfuls of sour cream, accompanied by crusty bread.

SERVES 4

$^1/_4$ cup sun-dried tomatoes, chopped

2 tbsp olive oil

$^1/_2$–1 tsp crushed dried chiles

2–3 garlic cloves, chopped

1 large onion, cut into small wedges

1 small celery root, cut into small chunks

8 oz/225 g carrots, sliced

8 oz/225 g new potatoes, scrubbed and cut into chunks

1 small acorn squash, seeded, peeled, and cut into small chunks, about 8 oz/225 g prepared weight

2 tbsp tomato paste

$1^1/_4$ cups vegetable stock

$2^1/_2$ cups canned Puy or green lentils, drained and rinsed

1–2 tsp hot paprika

few fresh sprigs of thyme

1 lb/450 g ripe tomatoes, coarsely chopped

to serve

sour cream

crusty bread

Spicy Vegetable Stew

Heat the oil in a large, heavy-bottom pan with a tight-fitting lid, and cook the onion, garlic, chile, and eggplant, stirring frequently, for 5–8 minutes, or until softened.

Add the ginger, cumin, coriander, and saffron and cook, stirring constantly, for 2 minutes. Bruise the cinnamon stick.

Add the cinnamon, squash, sweet potatoes, prunes, stock, and tomatoes to the pan and bring to a boil. Reduce the heat, then cover and simmer, stirring occasionally, for 20 minutes. Add the chickpeas to the pan and cook for an additional 10 minutes. Discard the cinnamon and serve garnished with the fresh cilantro.

SERVES 4

2 tbsp olive oil

1 red onion, finely chopped

2–4 garlic cloves, crushed

1 fresh red chile, seeded and sliced

1 eggplant, about 8 oz/225 g, cut into small chunks

small piece fresh ginger root, peeled and grated

1 tsp ground cumin

1 tsp ground coriander

pinch of saffron threads or $1/2$ tsp turmeric

1–2 cinnamon sticks

$1/2$–1 butternut squash, about 1 lb/450 g, peeled, seeded, and cut into small chunks

8 oz/225 g sweet potatoes, cut into small chunks

$1/2$ cup dried and pitted prunes

2–2$1/2$ cups vegetable stock

4 tomatoes, chopped

14 oz/400 g canned chickpeas, drained and rinsed

1 tbsp chopped fresh cilantro, to garnish

Chile Bean Stew

Heat the oil in a large, heavy-bottom pan with a tight-fitting lid, and cook the onion, garlic, and chiles, stirring frequently, for 5 minutes, or until softened. Add the kidney and cannellini beans and the chickpeas. Blend the tomato paste with a little of the stock and pour over the bean mixture, then add the remaining stock. Bring to a boil, then reduce the heat and simmer for 10–15 minutes.

Add the red bell pepper, tomatoes, fava beans, and pepper to taste and simmer for 15–20 minutes, or until all the vegetables are tender. Stir in the chopped cilantro.

Serve the stew topped with spoonfuls of sour cream and garnished with chopped cilantro and a pinch of paprika.

SERVES 4–6

2 tbsp olive oil

1 onion, chopped

2–4 garlic cloves, chopped

2 fresh red chiles, seeded and sliced

$1^2/_3$ cups canned kidney beans, drained and rinsed

$1^2/_3$ cups canned cannellini beans, drained and rinsed

$1^2/_3$ cups canned chickpeas, drained and rinsed

1 tbsp tomato paste

$3–3^3/_4$ cups vegetable stock

1 red bell pepper, seeded and chopped

4 tomatoes, coarsely chopped

$1^1/_2$ cups frozen or shelled fresh fava beans, thawed if frozen

pepper

1 tbsp chopped fresh cilantro

sour cream, to serve

to garnish

chopped fresh cilantro

pinch of paprika

Lentil & Rice Casserole

Place the lentils, rice, and vegetable stock in a large flameproof casserole and cook over low heat, stirring occasionally, for 20 minutes.

Add the leek, garlic, tomatoes and juice from the can, ground cumin, chili powder, garam masala, sliced bell pepper, broccoli, baby corn, and green beans to the casserole.

Bring the mixture to a boil, reduce the heat, cover, and simmer for an additional 10–15 minutes or until all the vegetables are tender.

Add the shredded basil and season with salt and pepper to taste.

Garnish with fresh basil sprigs and serve immediately.

SERVES 4

1 cup red lentils, rinsed

1/4 cup long-grain rice

5 cups vegetable stock

1 leek, cut into chunks

3 garlic cloves, crushed

14 oz/400 g canned chopped
  tomatoes

1 tsp ground cumin

1 tsp chili powder

1 tsp garam masala

1 red bell pepper, seeded and sliced

3 1/2 oz/100 g small broccoli florets

8 baby corn, halved lengthwise

2 oz/55 g green beans, halved

1 tbsp shredded fresh basil

salt and pepper

fresh basil sprigs, to garnish

Roasted Vegetables

Preheat the oven to 400°F/200°C. Brush an ovenproof dish with a little oil. Arrange the fennel, onions, tomatoes, eggplant, zucchini, and bell peppers in the dish and tuck the garlic cloves and rosemary sprigs among them. Drizzle with the remaining oil and season to taste with pepper.

Roast the vegetables in the preheated oven for 10 minutes.

Turn the vegetables over, return the dish to the oven, and roast for an additional 10–15 minutes, or until the vegetables are tender and beginning to turn golden brown.

Serve the vegetables straight from the dish or transfer to a warm serving platter. Serve immediately, with crusty bread, if you like, to soak up the juices.

SERVES 4

2 tbsp olive oil

1 fennel bulb, cut into wedges

2 red onions, cut into wedges

2 beefsteak tomatoes, cut into wedges

1 eggplant, thickly sliced

2 zucchini, thickly sliced

1 yellow bell pepper, seeded and cut into chunks

1 red bell pepper, seeded and cut into chunks

1 orange bell pepper, seeded and cut into chunks

4 garlic cloves

4 fresh rosemary sprigs

ground black pepper

crusty bread, to serve (optional)

Parmesan Cheese Risotto with Mushrooms

Heat the oil in a deep pan. Add the rice and cook over low heat, stirring constantly, for 2–3 minutes, until the grains are thoroughly coated in oil and translucent.

Add the garlic, onion, celery, and bell pepper and cook, stirring frequently, for 5 minutes. Add the mushrooms and cook for 3–4 minutes. Stir in the oregano.

Gradually add the hot stock, a ladleful at a time. Stir constantly and add more liquid as the rice absorbs each addition. Increase the heat to medium so that the liquid bubbles.

Cook for 20 minutes, or until all the liquid is absorbed and the rice is creamy. Add the sun-dried tomatoes, if using, 5 minutes before the end of the cooking time and season to taste with salt and pepper.

Remove the risotto from the heat and stir in half the Parmesan until it melts. Transfer the risotto to warmed bowls. Top with the remaining cheese, garnish with flat-leaf parsley or bay leaves, and serve at once.

SERVES 6

2 tbsp olive oil or vegetable oil

1 cup risotto rice

2 garlic cloves, crushed

1 onion, chopped

2 celery stalks, chopped

1 red or green bell pepper, seeded and chopped

8 oz/225 g button mushrooms, thinly sliced

1 tbsp chopped fresh oregano or 1 tsp dried oregano

4 cups boiling vegetable stock

$1/4$ cup sun-dried tomatoes in olive oil, drained and chopped (optional)

salt and pepper

$1/2$ cup finely grated Parmesan cheese

fresh flat-leaf parsley sprigs or bay leaves, to garnish